Cleopatra

Library of Congress Control Number: 2017957515
ISBN 978-1-250-16621-0

Our books may be purchased in bulk for promotional, educational, or business use.
Please contact your local bookseller or the Macmillan Corporate and Premium Sales Department
at (800) 221-7945 ext. 5442 or by e-mail at MacmillanSpecialMarkets@macmillan.com.

First published in France in 2014 by Quelle Histoire, Paris
First U.S. edition, 2018

Text: Patricia Crété
Translation: Catherine Nolan
Illustrations: Bruno Wennagel, Mathieu Ferret

Printed in China by RR Donnelley Asia Printing Solutions Ltd., Dongguan City, Guangdong Province
10 9 8 7 6 5 4 3 2 1

Cleopatra

Roaring Brook Press
New York

Birth of a Queen

Cleopatra was born in Alexandria, Egypt, more than two thousand years ago. She lived in a large palace with her family. Her father was the *pharaoh*, or ruler, of Egypt.

—

69 BCE

Childhood

Young Cleopatra was very bright. She did not go to school. Instead, she was taught by tutors at the palace. She learned to speak at least five different languages!

———

62 BCE

Power

When Cleopatra turned eighteen, her father named her queen.

In Egypt, women were not allowed to rule alone. Cleopatra had to share her power with her younger brother, Ptolemy.

Before long, Ptolemy decided he wanted all the power for himself. He sent Cleopatra away and began to rule Egypt on his own.

——

51 BCE

The Roman Empire

But another ruler had his eye on Egypt.

Julius Caesar was a great Roman general. He had helped Rome take over many lands and build a mighty empire. Now he planned to take over Egypt, too.

---

48 BCE

Caesar Meets Cleopatra

Caesar went to Alexandria to meet with Ptolemy. Ptolemy was angry. He didn't want to lose control of Egypt.

Cleopatra heard about Caesar's visit. She got an idea. What if she got Caesar on her side? But to do that, she would have to meet with him.

Cleopatra sneaked past her brother's guards into the palace, hidden inside a rolled-up carpet.

When Caesar saw Cleopatra, he fell in love with her!

―――

48 BCE

Off to Rome

Caesar and Cleopatra sailed to Rome together. They signed a peace treaty between Egypt and the Roman Empire.

They also had a child together, a son named Caesarion.

When Caesarion was three years old, Caesar was killed. Cleopatra went back to Alexandria with her little boy.

46–44 BCE

Return to Egypt

Cleopatra's brother, Ptolemy, had died. Now Cleopatra had to fight her other siblings for power. At last, she became the sole ruler of Egypt. She took over the throne with her son by her side.

A few years later, Cleopatra received an invitation. It was from a new Roman ruler, Mark Antony. He wanted to meet the kings and queens of the lands under his rule.

44–41 BCE

Mark Antony

Cleopatra arrived on a golden ship for her meeting with Mark Antony.

Now it was his turn to fall in love with her! Mark Antony and Cleopatra had three children.

Together, Cleopatra and Mark Antony ruled Egypt and the rest of the Roman Empire. But someone else wanted to take over—Caesar's adopted son, Octavian.

41–30 BCE

Battle at Sea

Octavian thought he was the rightful ruler of the Roman Empire. He went to war with Mark Antony and Cleopatra.

They waged a huge battle at sea. Cleopatra watched the battle from her royal ship. She saw how it was going to end. She and Mark Antony were about to be defeated.

———

31 BCE

The End

Cleopatra and Mark Antony fled to Alexandria. Octavian's soldiers followed them.

As the enemy approached, Mark Antony took his own life. Then Cleopatra took her own life, too. She let a poisonous snake bite her!

It was the end of an exciting life for Cleopatra, the very last queen of Egypt.

30 BCE

75 BCE

69 BCE
Birth of Cleopatra.

51 BCE
Cleopatra marries her brother Ptolemy XIII.

49 BCE
Ptolemy XIII sends Cleopatra to Syria.

48 BCE
Caesar arrives in Alexandria.

46 BCE
Caesar becomes ruler of the Roman Empire.

44 BCE
Caesar is killed by rivals.

51 BCE
Beginning of Cleopatra's reign.

47 BCE
Caesarion is born.

46 BCE
Caesar and Cleopatra go to Rome.

44 BCE
Cleopatra returns to Egypt with Caesarion.

37 BCE
Cleopatra and Mark Antony marry.

30 BCE
Octavian arrives in Alexandria with his soldiers.

30 BCE
Death of Cleopatra.

25 BCE

41 BCE
Mark Antony meets Cleopatra.

31 BCE
Octavian defeats Cleopatra and Mark Antony in a battle at sea.

30 BCE
Death of Mark Antony.

? | *Dates in this book are followed by the letters BCE. This means that the events took place before the Common Era began, or before year 1 of the calendar as we know it today.*

Egypt Before the Roman Conquest

MAP KEY

1 Alexandria, Egypt

This city was founded by Alexander the Great in the fourth century BCE. It was a well-to-do city, filled with monuments, including a lighthouse and a great library.

2 The Pyramids

These gigantic constructions were symbols of Egyptian power and knowledge. They also served as tombs for the pharaohs. No one is sure how the Egyptians built them.

3 The Nile River

This river is the longest one in Africa, measuring 4,258 miles.

4 The Battle of Pharsalus

Caesar won this battle against his rival Pompey to become the ruler of the Roman Empire.

5 Rome, Italy

According to legend, this city was founded by Remus and Romulus, two brothers descended from the god Mars. Rome became the center of a huge empire.

6 The Battle of Actium

Mark Antony and Octavian fought this naval battle on September 2, 31 BCE. Helped by his friend Agrippa, Octavian won the battle.

Egyptian Empire   **Roman Empire**

People to Know

Ptolemy XII
(117–51 BCE)
Cleopatra's father was the pharaoh of Egypt. He was nicknamed "the flute player."

Ptolemy XIII
(61–47 BCE)
Cleopatra's younger brother was about ten years old when he and Cleopatra ruled together. He pushed her out of power in 49 BCE and exiled her to Syria.

Julius Caesar
(100–44 BCE)
A brilliant student and good athlete, he started out in politics at an early age. After he took power in Rome, he was killed by his rivals.

Agrippa
(63 BCE–12 CE)
Agrippa was an excellent soldier. He helped Octavian win the Battle of Actium and become the emperor of the Roman Empire.

....

....

Cleopatra and her brother Ptolemy XIII were not the only ones fighting for control of Egypt. Their younger brother, Ptolemy XIV, also ruled with Cleopatra for a time. Their sister Arsinoe fought against them for the throne.

Cleopatra was not actually Egyptian. Her ancestors came from Macedonian Greece and all spoke Greek. Cleopatra was the first in her line to learn the Egyptian language.

Cleopatra married two of her brothers. This was the custom at the time.

Roman women imitated Cleopatra's hairstyle and her pearl jewelry. Her style became so popular that researchers today can't always tell which statues are supposed to be Cleopatra and which ones are Roman ladies copying their queen.